I thank the Lord for all he *has* done for me. I thank the Lord for all he *is* doing for me, and I thank the Lord for all he *will be* doing.

"Seek the Kingdom of God above all else, and live righteously, and he will give you everything you need. (Matthew 6:33)

Sincerely,

CP, The Girl with The Notebook

If they will shenan
once, they will
shenanigan

@librasgetlaid

YUP BECAUSE...

A hooler is going to hooligan.

@therhodyjean

Never trust Chris.
Because if Chris
crossed Applesauce,
what do you think he
is going to do to you?

@reyofsunshine76

If you want to mess around with X, Y, Z just make sure you minus me.

@ _obeythebri2

You couldn't protect anything! Even if you died and came back a condom.

@Ms.Understood

I swear to the strap on Jesus left sandal, if I bite into something thinking its chicken and it's a mushroom... I am swinging.

@_obeythebri2

The bible says to forgive 70 times 7 which is 490

On 491, I am swinging.

@Sarye'Ah Williams

Well call me a pair of overalls, cause I am over all over your .....

@Aaron Down

You like white boys for real? Or are you going to call me a sour cream citizen when you get mad?

@Tommy Lee

You should have seen me and your mama when we were young. We were wilder than two spoons in the dishwasher.

@justinstagner

Just so you
know, the back
might be big, but
the back still
gets bent.

@_obeythebri2

The key to settling any dispute in marriage is simply asking your wife to sit on your face so you can see where she's coming from

@Steve Wiltz

One thing about me is I put the "no" in I will let you know... cause it's a no for me.

@ Ashlee_ruth

I am asking you clear questions and you are giving me cloudy answers.

@Fatboyzkitchenla

Slap me on a
penny because
we are not
Lincoln.

- unknown.

I went out to
have drinks, but
the drinks
wound up
having me.

@comedy bae

I do not feel bonita. I feel like I'm sweating tequila.

@ashlee_ruth

I am about to
use y=mx+b to
figure out the
slope of the line
you just crossed

@Ali

I might be built
like a
playstation, but
you can't play
me.

@Littlerockyae

Don't get me wrong, I am all for feral girl fall but I've been having a little bit more of a rock bottom autumn.

@Ashlee_ruth

Hamburger freaking
help me!

@veteran mortgage
warrior

Folks swear
they be putting 2
and 2 together.
How about you
put 5 and 5
together and 10
to your business.

@shannon

Mind the business that pays you sugar, because you do not work for me.

@ssg2015

If I wanted to hear
from an asshole, I
would have farted.

@Khadeeja Morse
RMS

If it were raining
brains, your ass
would not get wet.

@Hoodrat2Harvard

If I find out my little 'yeah' is out here 'yeah-ing' on another "yeah", I am going to "aight".

@Yall Know Q

If they ghost
you, respect the
dead and move
on.

@Don't Trip

It happens to be hotter than a spoon in a crack house out here.

@southern_drawl_yall

I am pretty sure that shrek is in my shorts arguing with my ass about whose swap it is.

@Rey Rey

Listen, it is hotter than two squirrels porking in a wool sock outside right now.

@cactustate

If your family didn't want you to air out the dirty laundry, maybe they would have given you clean clothes to wear.

@Ginger Jack

We are the napping generation. One thing we prioritize is a nap. We take a nap before we go to sleep. We have a nap before bed.

@Pocaspeakss

Don't date them if you aint their type because their types probably your friend. That chapter should have been closed, why the heck did it begin?

@sa.tomaa

You're not going to be an acquired taste to everybody. It's not your fault their palette is not prepared for fine dining.

@A.love8

Rip me off your
roster, you been
playing games boo
but you ain't know
that I got options, I
been playing games
too.

@Arleisham

If we break up today, you get replaced today. I ain't sick, I don't need time to heal.

@daacoldestmortician

On the deadest of asses. On the frankest of Benjamins and the greenest of beans... can you please tell me why you are so mean?

@Coliehutzler

Roses are Red, Rivers they flow. There are so many ways to hell, just pick one and go.

@Iamleahbrody

Roses are red, it aint
no cheese without the
mac, cheers to life
whooping our ass but
at least we're fighting
back

@ Myron Tillman

Okay, you did your
big one but whose
back is bigger, MINE!
So that means I am
going to come back
with a bigger one.

@cessikali

If you think I'm about to sit up and argue with you...well you're absolutely right! If you want silence, go to a library.

@nairabills

Them: Oh, what do you look for in a man?

Me: Well, I look away!

@imo_unusual

Take the L out of
Lover brother,
because is Over.

@itsvickiemae

Them: Oh, you don't hit me up anymore.

Me: The phone is bisexual! It goes both ways.

@lilberated

They always said don't bring sand to the beach, but they never said nothing about bringing the drip to the water.

@everyonesaweirdo

If your waiter can overflow your cup like this. Imagine what God can do.

@creatorcarlton

"A voice of one calling: "in the wilderness prepare the way for the Lord; make straight in the desert a highway for our God."

Isaiah 40:3 (NIV)

ACKNOWLEDGMENTS

Thank you to everyone from social media who follows The Girl With The Notebook. If your social media name is cited in this book, a special thanks to you guys!

I would like anyone who reads this book to go and follow each one of the poets.

I wanted to take a moment and personally,

acknowledge each person.

SPECIAL SHOUT OUT!

Follow everyone on who is cited in this GOLD BOOK on social media.

@librasgetlaid

@therhodyjean

@reyofsunshine76

@ _obeythebri2

@Ms.Understood

@Sarye'Ah Williams

@Aaron Down

@Tommy Lee

@justinstagner

@Steve Wiltz

@Ashlee_ruth

@Ali

@Littlerockyae

@Fatboyzkitchenla

@comedy bae

**Unknown (slap me
on a penny lady)**

**@veteran mortgage
warrior**

@shannon

@ssg2015

@Khadeeja Morse
RMS

@Hoodrat2Harvard

@Yall Know Q

@Don't Trip

@southern_drawl_yall

@Rey Rey

@cactustate

@Ginger Jack

@Pocaspeakss

@sa.tomaa

@A.love8

@Arleisham

@daacoldestmortician

@Coliehutzler

@Iamleahbrody

@ Myron Tillman

@cessikali

@nairabills

@imo_unusual

@itsvickiemae

@lilberated

@everyonesaweirdo

@creatorcarlton

"But you, Lord are a shield around me, my glory, the One who lifts my head high."

-Psalms 3:3

NEVER STOP BELIEVING AND HAVING FAITH IN THE LORD. IT IS NEVER HOW IT SEEMS.

I am living proof that if you put God first in all you do, God will show up and show OUT! I never thought this would be happening in a million years but ...GOD!

Today is better than yesterday and tomorrow will be better than today.

Trust the process.

Trust in the Lord with all your heart and lean not on your own understanding; in all your ways submit to him, and he will make your paths straight.

Proverbs 3: 5-6

THANK YOU TO MY FAMILY, MY CHURCH, AND FRIENDS.

I love all of you will the love of God.

Sincerely,
The Girl with The
Book

Made in the USA
Columbia, SC
16 February 2025

53923846R00042